# SAN DIEGO

# SAN DIEGO

Text by
## PETER JENSEN

Photography by
## BILL ROSS
## CRAIG AURNESS
## WEST LIGHT

**SKYLINE PRESS**

Produced by Roger Boulton Publishing Services, Toronto
Designed by Fortunato Aglialoro

©Oxford University Press (Canadian Branch) 1984
SKYLINE PRESS is a registered imprint of the Oxford University Press

ISBN 0-19-540603-6
1 2 3 4 - 7 6 5 4
Printed in Hong Kong by Scanner Art Services, Inc., Toronto

Plates 22, 24, 26, 35, 47, 55, 56, 76, from photography
by Craig Aurness. All other photography by Bill Ross.

# INTRODUCTION

It was a 75-degree winter day in San Diego. The warm Santa Ana winds were blowing lazily off the desert and out to sea. Palm trees rustled their skirts like swaying fan dancers beneath a cloudless blue sky. On the horizon the Coronado Islands were clearly visible in the dry air after hiding for weeks behind ocean haze. Downtown new mirrored towers glittered amidst the tile roofs and arches of San Diego's older Mission Revival buildings and the world's largest fleet of tuna boats set up a sort of waterfront fence of bristling masts.

High atop Point Loma, at the Cabrillo National Monument—site of the Portuguese navigator Juan Rodríguez Cabrillo's first contact with San Diego Bay in 1542, a man in a San Diego Padres baseball cap swept his binoculars across the scene, picking out landmarks 30 miles away.

'This is why I live in San Diego,' he said, turning to his companions. 'It was so nice this morning that I wanted to do a little of everything—run on the beach, picnic beside El Prado in Balboa Park, take a sailboat out on Mission Bay, or just stay home and garden. Life's tough in Paradise, isn't it?'

Whether it's admiring a stunning day, revelling in a sunset, or becoming indignant when a morning layer of fog hangs near the coast too long, such reactions are all part of life in San Diego. This weather-watching is equivalent in a San Diegan to a Midwestern farmer talking about rainfalls and freezes. Weather dominates the region by its near-perfection. It has always impressed and attracted visitors, from the first wanderers—the San Dieguito Indians—around 10,000 BC, to a doctor in the late 1800s who went so far as to say that 'The inhabitants have secured a large stock of thermometers and pulviometers and have zealous meteorologists, and are determined to demonstrate the unparalleled sanitary values of their growing burgh.' His spiel worked—thousands came to San Diego solely to improve their health.

Photographers, also, have been impressed. There is nothing quite like San Diego light, be it slanting across the Laguna Mountains, a high range that separates San Diego from the desert, or dropping its salmon-colored curtains into the West's unbroken horizon. Photographers find images at every turn.

San Diego is a large city that covers about 300 square miles and in population it is now the eighth metropolis in the United States. Spurts of growth have gripped the area several times since Franciscan Father Junipero Serra founded Mission San Diego de Alcalá in 1769—so laying the anchor of the California mission chain. Early explorers could see at once that the land surrounding the harbor Cabrillo had discovered was perfect for settlement. It consisted of low and fairly flat mesas, cut by perennial streams running to the sea. One great valley unfolded eastward from the bay, following the course of the San Diego River. It would host the first serious settlements in the area under the typical Spanish three-part plan of colonization in the New World—establish a mission, a presidio, and a pueblo, and don't forget to look for gold.

Throughout the Spanish and Mexican eras of development, San Diego's residents clustered around the garrison on a hillside above the San Diego River. Eventually a town grew up around a small dusty plaza (literally jumping with fleas), while out near Point Loma the smell led to cowhide houses that traded with ships out of Boston. Much of San Diego's growth was coming from an influx of foreigners (even mountain man Jedediah Smith came through in 1826). They mixed, not always comfortably, with the governing *Mexicanos*.

War between the United States and Mexico in 1846 signalled the end of Mexican rule in San Diego and emphasis soon shifted to Yankee settlement of what was called New Town several miles to the south (the site of today's downtown). A central figure in the boom of

1868 was Alonzo Horton, who parcelled up almost 1,000 acres in and near downtown and saw 226 blocks sell off in a matter of months. Old Town was all but forgotten, with many of its adobe structures crumbling to earthen mounds. Some of the houses remain today though, as part of Old Town State Historic Park, including the restored Casa de Estudillo, one of California's finest courtyard homes from the Mexican period.

Despite the efforts of developer-genius Horton and others after him, San Diego remained just a little further down the railroad line than Los Angeles and always a few steps behind its northern neighbor in growth and commerce (blessedly so, for San Diego has avoided, up to now, much of the sprawl and congestion plaguing Los Angeles). After World War II, growth accelerated again as many veterans who'd shipped out for Pacific duty from San Diego returned to Southern California. The military, especially the US Navy, strengthened its 11th Fleet operations out of San Diego to the point where this became a 'navy town', and it was assumed that a San Diegan must be connected to the military in some way—at least through someone in the family.

Life was good up on the mesas. Row upon row of small houses lined the canyon rims, many with eclectic little gardens growing everything from banana plants and cactus to limes and lemons. The beaches, having started with the first heyday of tent cities in Coronado, continued to be a summer-long attraction and cottages shouldered their way into the sandy strip that separated the surf from Mission Bay. Tourism came into its own when Mission Bay was dredged to create a huge playland for small boats bordered by parks and hotels. The city's growth was shifting almost imperceptibly to the north and once again Mission Valley, only steps from the first houses of the *padres*, was the focus. Downtown languished, its major retail stores drawn to the new shopping centers in the valley, its office buildings squat and dreary.

Today, 20 years after the retail exodus began, downtown is back in favor again. Millions of square feet of office space are opening up in bold new towers, and a downtown shopping center named for Horton is the key to center-city redevelopment. After years of not having an outdoor restaurant or sidewalk café, downtown is aswirl with pedestrians munching hotdogs at vendors' carts, sipping espresso at small tables beneath tassled umbrellas and strolling the waterfront promenades of Seaport Village—a Disneyesque collection of shops and restaurants on San Diego Harbor. Where you once would have expected to find a smelly cannery, the new Hotel Intercontinental's gleaming ellipse rises like a sail above the shipyards.

The Gaslamp Quarter, all that remains of Horton's New Town, is struggling back from being skid row to become a historic district with newly bricked sidewalks, offices, shops, and restaurants. Artists have moved into lofts wherever they can find them south of Market, often putting up with the hum of sewing machines from garment factories above and below, while more than a dozen art galleries have opened in the last two years.

The city is *alive* again, thank you, and unlike most urban centers it keeps a small-town feeling, amidst the steel and glass, so that it's usual for an office worker to run into an acquaintance at lunch and to greet shopowners and waiters by name. Old haunts are being replaced by new, just as steak sandwiches gave way recently to pasta, salads and sushi.

Through it all runs an almost invisible thread that ties the city, after 225 years, to Mexico. At times the whole relationship twists into a Gordian knot. The Mexico–US border area is one of San Diego's greatest tourist assets, yet it is plagued by illegal immigration and a lack of fundamental city services, such as adequate sewage treatment, on the Mexico side. Tijuana (no, it is not called Ti-*a*-wana) is a vibrant city full of colors never seen on buildings north of the border, *mercados* bursting with tropical fruits, citrus, birds in bamboo cages, *piñatas*, and beggar children selling Chiclets. *Panaderias* (bakeries) fill the air with the aroma of fresh-baked *bolillos* (crusty rolls), and wonderful restaurants serve a cuisine quite unlike the 'Mexican' food (the too-familiar ground-beef tacos, beans, and rice) found north of the border. The 'Line' is like a cultural tidal zone surging daily with commerce and tourism, mixing poverty with prosperity. Typical of the dichotomy is the news that recently, with little fanfare, Tijuana's millions passed San Diego in population size—yet over half the city's houses do not have running water.

The tourists' San Diego is richer than ever. At the Zoo, new animal habitats include an open primate area where visitors walk on aerial platforms to stand at eye level with chimps in the treetops. In Wild Animal Park, a zoo without cages, the birth rate among free-roaming animals is astoundingly high. Sea World's new Penguin Encounter, a frigid aquarium for serious ornithological study, is every bit as popular as their circus-like whale and dolphin shows. Balboa Park, originally set aside by city planners in 1868 while Horton's tract was selling off, is a mature park of grand buildings strung out along El Prado; a promenade built for the Panama–California Exposition, 1915-16. Behind the richly decorated facades are museums and exhibit halls, and you have a wide choice from anthropology to Cézanne, from model train exhibits to the photography of Diane Arbus.

Above all, this is a water city where you can skin-dive, deep-sea fish, surf, waterski, skipper a Hobie Cat, windsurf, jetski, waterski, canoe, crew. Pick any imaginable water sport, and it's bound to be a year-round activity on San Diego's saltwater (and on dozens of inland reservoirs). This is a city of fitness buffs, and the sport of triathlon (where contestants swim in the ocean, bike-ride, and run over marathon distances consecutively) started when an athletic club on Mission Bay dreamed up the 'Ironman' concept. San Diegans *know* how to play.

San Diegans' favorite Sunday drive (or bicycle ride) is along the coast highway northward from Pacific Beach. La Jolla, the 'jewel' of golden cliffs laced with caves, has grown from a few cottages and hotels above the coves to become San Diego's most prestigious address—both for homes and office buildings. Whatever the changing nature of the town, out in the water, floating a few feet above the submerged, grass-bearded reefs, snorkelers find peace—and hope for a glimpse of bright orange garibaldi fish.

Interstate highways crisscross the city and county and are comparatively free of the bumper-to-bumper coagulation that seizes up other cities. In one extraordinary stretch near downtown, Interstate 5 passes under the flight path for the airport and the incoming jets look as if they're about to leave skid marks on your car's roof. These highways open up San Diego's incredible diversity, from the flower fields of North County, draped like banners across the hillsides, to the old mining town of Julian in the Cuyamaca backcountry. This is a big place and no one can see it in a few days or even a week. Those with orderly prioritized schedules will only cry out in frustration; at every turn there is something to trap you for a day of pleasure rather than just an hour of looking around.

To be sure, there is some trouble in Paradise. Bulldozers graze the canyons like big, geometrically minded sheep, terracing the land into a Mayan look for new housing subdivisions. Dozens of citizen groups go before City Council each year in protest; some of them succeed in having canyons set aside as urban wilderness preserve. S.O.H.O. (Save Our Heritage Organization) and the San Diego Historical Society have been models for the rest of the country, preserving many of San Diego's finest buildings. But they've also lost out often, among their losses being a few works of Irving Gill, the city's internationally known architect of the early 1900s. Downtown you're apt to see a rumpled street-denizen sleeping in a Market Street doorway, as you head for one of the city's lovely little theaters.

You expect these things of any city but somehow in San Diego you suspect they are also avoidable. It wasn't campaign rhetoric that prompted a mayor (now US Senator Pete Wilson) to proclaim San Diego 'America's Finest City'. San Diegans believe it, and they aren't about to be caught 'just passing through'. Sometimes a certain neurosis sets in, prompting bumper stickers such as 'Welcome to San Diego! Now go home.' But for the most part it is pride, not smugness, that powers this city's personality.

It's something simpler, also, than the politics and economics of urban life. It may be the feel of sand shifting between your toes on Torrey Pines beach. It may be breakfasting on your patio in December, or stopping at a strawberry stand in March. You might swim out past the surfline at sunset to be closer to the pelicans doing their crumpled-wing dives for dinner. This place called San Diego is, in the end, like sable against skin—natural, warm, and very, very comforting.

San Diego, March 1984                      PETER JENSEN

1  San Diego Bay, sunrise

Small boats cluster around the margins of Shelter Island—actually a peninsula of parks, marinas, and hotels. Twin hangers at the Coronado Naval Air Station catch the dawn's first rays, while downtown still rests in shadow.

**2** *(left)* Coronado's Silver Strand

Condominiums line a narrow isthmus just south of Coronado's grand Hotel 'Del', more properly the Hotel del Coronado, built in 1888. The hotel's peaked-roof boathouse, now restored as a restaurant, sits like a little wedding cake amidst the Coronado Yacht Club sailboats.

**3** Bell Tower, Mission San Diego de Alcalá

Father Serra founded the first of California's Franciscan missions on Presidio Hill, San Diego, in 1769 and five years later the mission moved to the present site. Since then fire, earthquake, and in the last century generations of neglect required several reconstructions of this graceful, white-washed church with its five-bell tower. The name of the mission was given in honour of Saint Didacus of Alcalá in Spain. Indirectly this is the original of the city's name also—indirectly only because the site of the future city was named in 1602 by Sebastian Vizcaíno after his flagship, which he had already named after the Spanish saint.

Here aloes lift up their 'red hot pokers' in January outside the mission walls.

4  *(left)* Tuna fleet at anchor, San Diego Bay

A forest of cables, rope ladders, masts and trees stands silhouetted against the sunset along Harbor Drive. A mixed grove of palm trees and seafaring technology. Most of the city's palms were planted in the first decades after 1900, when a sort of botanical fever, led by Kate Sessions, gripped the city. Sophisticated electronic gear still hasn't replaced the classic crow's nests used to spot feeding schools of fish.

5  Sunset from Quail Botanical Gardens

Multitrunk eucalyptus trees cage the horizon high on a hill in Encinitas, where a small botanical garden abounds with exotic plants.

6  *(left)* La Jolla Cove

Pockets of sand collect along La Jolla's rocky coast. The protected cove is a favorite with snorkelers who flipper out a few dozen yards to grassy reefs.

7  The *Star of India*, Maritime Museum

Sails set, but anchored forever along the Embarcadero, the *Star of India* is the oldest steel-hulled sailing ship afloat. Behind her is the ferryboat *Berkeley* and the steam yacht *Media*, all part of the Maritime Museum.

8  Downtown San Diego from Shelter Island

Viewed from atop the Sheraton Harbor Island Hotel, downtown's towers
are still ablaze with lights just after sunset. A riverboat turned restaurant
is just distinguishable at the causeway's end.

9  Seaport Village

A waterfront development within walking distance of downtown, Seaport Village is an amalgam of New England, Western, and Mediterranean-style architecture, housing shops and restaurants.

10  Point Loma cliffs, high tide

Geologic strata have been stripped back by waves at the entrance to San Diego Bay. Tidepoolers can venture 100 yards or more from the base of the cliffs at low tide.

11  *(right)* Community Concourse in downtown San Diego

Downtown's Community Concourse (built in the mid-1960s) is a mix of city offices, Civic Theater (shown here), sculpture and fountain, and a convention center. At noon, the plaza is a gathering place for office workers basking in the sun.

**12** *(left)* Point Loma and the entrance to San Diego Bay

Juan Rodríguez Cabrillo rounded these rugged scarps on 28 September 1542 and sailed into a calm, estuarine bay. Today the Point is one of America's most popular National Monuments in terms of visitor numbers (the main attraction is the spectacular view). The old lighthouse, a lone white building, can be seen at the Point's summit.

**13** Hotel Del Coronado

San Diego's great Victorian lady, the Hotel 'Del', has been a symbol of tourist luxury since it was built in 1888 and is the last surviving Victorian resort of its kind in California. The octagonal roof-crown, a masterpiece of wooden construction, shelters several ballrooms and restaurants.

14  Mission San Luis Rey de Francia, east of Oceanside

A day's horseback ride north of Mission San Diego de Alcalá and midway between San Diego and San Juan Capistrano, this 'the King of the Missions' was founded in 1789 and named after Louis XI of France. It was the largest of the missions, with a church that could hold a thousand people.

15  *(right)* Heritage Park

These houses were moved here by conservationists from around the city as the wrecker's ball threatened and in this way a new neighborhood was created on a hill above Old Town State Historic Park.

16 Tortilla making in Old Town

*Masa*, corn softened in limewater and then stone ground, is patted by hand to make the traditional Mexican *tortilla*. Demonstration at Bazaar del Mundo in Old Town takes place on weekends.

17 Posada ceremony, Mission San Luis Rey
The holy family's journey to Bethlehem is recreated at parish churches each Christmastide in San Diego's Latin communities. Both of the missions in San Diego County still serve congregations.

18  *(left)* Tuna boats on the Embarcadero

Twin empty tuna seiners, floating high in the water, await their first trip. The tuna industry, severely depressed in the 1980s, is beset by boundary disputes in foreign waters as captains range their boats further and further from San Diego, often following warm-water currents down the coast of South America.

19  Spiral stairway, Point Loma lighthouse

Like the inside of a chambered shell, tower stairs invite National Monument visitors up to look at the lighthouse's beveled Fresnel lens.

20 Sculpture, high-tech office complex
*Stargazer* by Alexander Lieberman shoots skyward from the grounds of the San Diego Tech Center, one of many new research and development office parks in the Sorrento Valley area, north of downtown San Diego.

21 *(right)* San Diego Trolley
Linking downtown with the San Ysidro–Tijuana border crossing since 1982, the bright-red 'trolley' (actually a state-of-the-art German-made electric train) is a new lightrail transit system laid out over old railroad rights of way.

22  *(left)* Chart House Restaurant, Coronado
One of the city's most picturesque buildings
was once the Hotel 'Del' boathouse. Yachters
can anchor nearby and row over for famous
steak-and-lobster dinners.

23  Broadway and the financial district
Strings of stoplights flash on San Diego's
major downtown thoroughfare. City blocks
are small, and most of the streets narrow.

24  Armed Forces Day, Broadway Pier

On weekends, a Navy ship usually ties up to the Broadway Pier and opens to the public. Armed Forces Day brings the added spectacle of Navy bands and color reviews.

25  *(right)* U.C.S.D. Library

The late San Diego architectural critic James Britton described this library, designed by the William Pereira group, as 'hovering for all the world like an intelligence-stocked spaceship from a better planet.'

26 Neon reflections, Gaslamp Quarter
Gaslamp theatre marquees create a gaudy display of color along Fifth Avenue in what is for the most part a district of historic buildings.

27 *(right)* Pacific Beach
Scallops of retreating waves etch a beach widened by summer's deposits of sand. In winter, much of the coastline is stripped down to its rock-bed by storm waves.

28 *(left)* Ranunculus fields, Encinitas

The cool coastal climate zone in Encinitas on the county's north coast is ideal for growing flowers—for cuttings, nursery stock, and seed. Here a tour group discovers why Encinitas is called by local promoters 'The Flower Capital of the World'.

29 La Jolla and Children's Pool Beach

The curving seawall was built at the turn of the century to create a safe, shallow, wading pool for children. Today this is mostly dry beach, but is still a favorite haven for families with toddlers. The bulky condominium tower helped precipitate laws limiting highrise buildings so close to the coast.

30  Wild Animal Park, San Pasqual Valley

San Diego Wild Animal Park near Escondido is an extension of the San Diego Zoo—with a big difference; animals roam across a huge, almost indiscernibly fenced area of hillsides and plains. Visitors tour from veldt to rain forest on a monorail. In the main compound area, primates clamber up eucalyptus trunks next to a restaurant patio, manmade lakes, and amphitheaters featuring trained animal shows.

31 Ocotillo plant, Anza-Borrego

Twisted limbs of ocotillo will turn a bright orange in spring with thousands of tiny petalled flowers set amidst the spikes.

32 *(left)* Harbor Island Marina

San Diego Bay's marshy edges were dredged to create a huge small-boat marina. The city is called home by some of the world's best sailors, including America's Cup captain Dennis Connor.

33 La Jolla shoreline

Layered rocks, an Upper Cretaceous formation typical of the shoreline from Point Loma to La Jolla, are part of the coastal terrace laid bare by the waves.

**34 Shorefishing, San Diego Bay**

Although known for its offshore sportfishing, San Diego has a cadre of shorefishermen who line the tiny beaches and breakwaters of San Diego and Mission bays. Behind this pair stands the Sheraton Harbor Island Hotel.

**35** *(right)* San Diego-Coronado Bridge

The long, languid curve of the 'Blue Bridge' is the city's strongest architectural statement. It changes hue throughout the day, or simply stands in bold silhouette, as in this sunrise photograph.

36  *(left)* Palomar Observatory

The great dome has been rotated once during this one-hour-long exposure made at night, showing one of the world's largest stargazers—the 200-inch Hale Telescope.

37  Skyline at night

The stepped crown of the Columbia Center is one of the newest additions to the skyline. Tower heights are limited by the nearby flightpath of Lindbergh Field.

**38 Lily pond and Conservatory, Balboa Park**

The lath conservatory houses exotic plants, including a collection of bromeliads and epiphyllums. The lily pond, just off El Prado, is a favorite gathering place for artists and strolling musicians.

**39** *(right)* **Cap'n'Kid's World, Sea World Amusement Park**

'That's me! And me! And me!' she wonders at the children's playground section of a park famous for its marine mammal shows, lushly landscaped grounds, and aquaria.

**40** *(left)* Aerospace Museum, Balboa Park

A dash of Streamline Moderne fountains and light fixtures at what was once the Ford Building at the California-Pacific Exposition in 1935. The San Diego firm, Ryan Aeronautical, built Lindbergh's *Spirit of St Louis*, memorialized by exhibits inside.

**41** *Eucalyptus pulruvienta*

Eucalyptus trees are perhaps the most prevalent trees in San Diego. Introduced from Australia in the 19th century to provide wood for railroad ties, the eucalyptus has adapted well to the San Diego climate.

42 Parking structure ramps, Downtown

Spiral ramps twist upward to create a center atrium in Community Concourse parking structure.

43 *(right)* Scripps Institute of Marine Biology Aquarium

San Diego coastal underwater habitats are recreated at the research institute's small aquarium in La Jolla. Visitors can see here what they'll encounter snorkeling in La Jolla Cove.

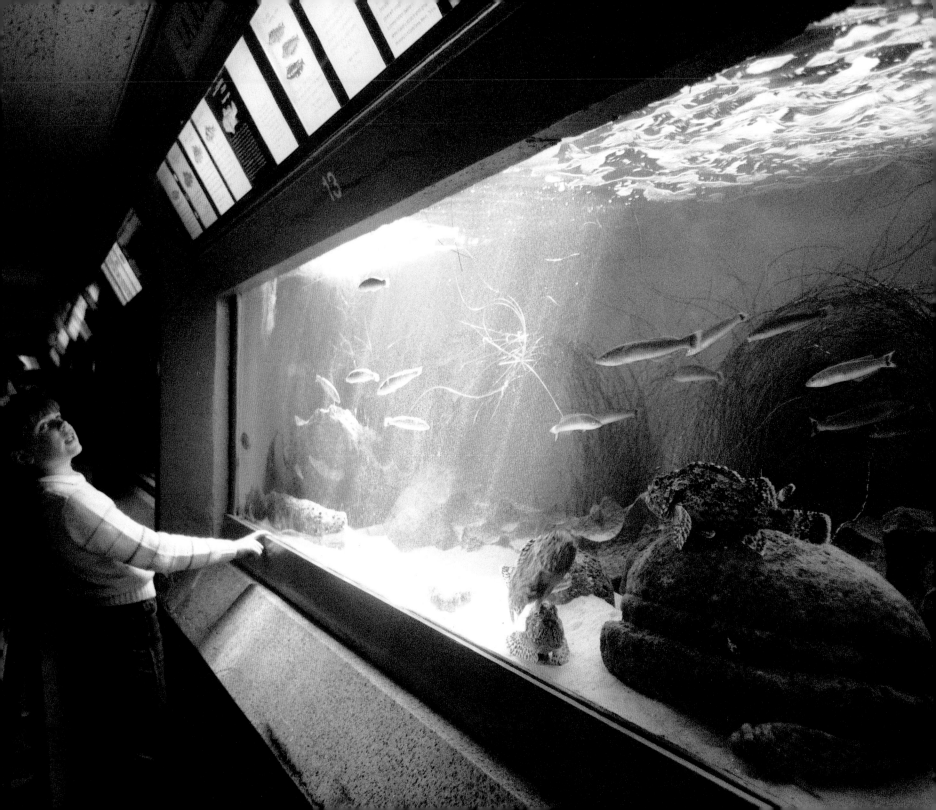

**44** San Diego Museum of Art

The museum's ornate facade is seen through another exposure of one of the two-story banners that hang to the sides of the entrance. Permanent collections range from Renaissance to contemporary and include a number of sculpture masterpieces placed in a small, tree-shaded sculpture garden. Nearby is the Old Globe Theatre.

**45** *(right)* La Jolla Caves

Waves follow weak points in the rock, undermining the La Jolla shoreline. One cave can only be reached by walking down a narrow, dimly lit tunnel dug beneath a curio and shell shop—not for the claustrophobic!

**46 Sunset cliffs**

Magnificent walls of sedimentary rock between Point Loma and Ocean Beach, seen here in the golden light of late afternoon.

**47** *(right)* **Tuna nets, Embarcadero**

Mountainous piles of nets await repair and reloading on the docks along Harbor Drive. Nets have been modified in recent years to reduce the number of porpoises entangled and drowned in the fishing haul.

48 Scripps Pier

The world-renowned oceanographic research center's pier stretches out past the surf-line to service some of the University of California's vessels. In the background, residential areas of La Jolla.

49 *(right)* Dolphin show, Sea World

Underwater signals send dolphins through their acrobatic maneuvers at one of Sea World's many saltwater pools that are fed by the waters of Mission Bay.

50  Silver Strand condominiums

Seen from the ocean side, highrise residences bask in the afternoon sun; visitors scramble on the rock breakwater in front of the Hotel Del Coronado. The Coronado peninsula is also the site of a navy training school, so that a beach adjacent to the southernmost luxury tower is the training ground for the élite Naval underwater demolition teams.

51  San Diego Museum of Art

Most ornate of the buildings constructed for the 1915–16 Panama-
California Exposition, the Museum of Man's facade is reminiscent of
Mexico's great cathedrals. Inside is an extensive collection of American
Indian artefacts. Shows range from shamanism to Halloween hauntings.

## 52  Badland Caves, Anza-Borrego

The desert is a place of discovery and surprise. Here, in a land of little water, caves cut by sudden rainfalls and flashflooding over thousands of years wend their way beneath the Badland Hills.

## 53  (right) Aerial view of Torrey Pines Cliffs

Table Rock juts from the shoreline beneath the state reserve; clearly it is almost an island. This formation is sometimes called Bathtub Rock, on account of a mysterious tub-sized depression filled with tidewater—dug out, some say, by a crazy coal miner.

54  Chicano Park, Barrio Logan

Concrete ramps to the Coronado Bridge became 'canvases' for local
Chicano artists after the freeways cut through their neighborhood. Now
the murals are the pride of the *barrio*.

55 Horton Plaza fountain

Three-quarters of a century old and still flowing, the fountain is the historic center of downtown. The Plaza area is now the site of a massive redevelopment project involving a multiblock shopping center, theaters and hotels.

56 California Tower, Balboa Park

A New York architect, Bertram Grosvenor Goodhue, brought his magic to the Panama-California Exposition of 1915–16 and San Diego has never looked the same since. Goodhue himself planned that most of the buildings with their temporary false fronts would be torn down to make way for gardens, but the structures, including this landmark tower, proved too endearing to San Diegans.

57 *(right)* Serra Museum, Presidio Park above Old Town

Often mistaken by tourists for Mission San Diego de Alcalá, Serra Museum crowns a hill near the intersection of Interstates 8 and 5 and is home to the San Diego Historical Society. Nearby is the site of the original Spanish presidio.

58 Anza-Borrego looking toward Mount Laguna

The nation's largest state park presents geology on a monumental scale—fault zones, granitic rocks of the Southern California batholith, and flash-flood washes.

59 *(right)* Tuna seiner off Point Loma

As a squall line approaches, a lone tuna seiner heads for harbor around Point Loma. The boats have a distinctive silhouette—high bow and low stern.

60 Palm Canyon, Anza-Borrego

Despite summertime temperatures on the valley floor over 110 degrees, Palm Canyon's creek flows year-round (except in severe drought). An hour's walk from park headquarters, native fan-palms clump at the water's edge. Their trunks were once blackened by fire but now the grove is carefully protected.

61  Vacation Village, Mission Bay

A hotel complex of lakes, pools, and bungalows occupies one of Mission
Bay's islands. Guests can waterski or sail only steps away from their
rooms.

62  *(left)* Mission Beach

High density, high rent. Life shoulder-to-shoulder in the beach communities is thought of as an advantage by many of 'M.B.'s' free spirits. Every house is within two blocks of beach or bay, and some of the city's most outlandish architecture punctuates the sandy boardwalks.

63 'Wall-to-wall' pleasure boats fill the marina at Harbor Island.

**64** *(left)* Downtown reflections

The Crocker Bank Building, as seen reflected in a neighboring tower on Broadway.

**65** Tiled Dome, Santa Fe Depot

Reminiscent in its style of the mission heritage, downtown's depot is on the National Register of Historic Places. Recent restoration has the old tile gleaming again, especially when seen against the backdrop of a glass curtain wall. The building's outdoor waiting room is gone, but the remainder is still very much unchanged.

66 *(left)* Interstate Highway 5 at sunset

Flowing bands of light against a typically pink sunset sky, Interstate 5 and the First Street bridge mark the northwest edge of downtown. The freeway at this point swings east, then south towards the border in a tight S-curve around the city's heart.

67 Fat City Restaurant, Pacific Coast Highway

Restauranteur Tom Fat, descendant of Chinese laborers who came to California during the 1849 Gold Rush, turned San Diego on its ear with his neon interpretation of an Art Deco theme. Fat City serves continental cuisine, while a companion restaurant in the same building, China Camp, offers 'California-Chinese' fare.

68 Old Globe Theatre, Balboa Park

Home of the San Diego Shakespeare Festival, the Old Globe was rebuilt after a tragic fire. The house is rarely without a performance and brings a wide range of drama to San Diego theatregoers.

69 Suburban development, La Jolla area

As San Diego's growth spreads in three directions (only the ocean can stop the inevitable and then only on one side), new neighborhoods of single and multifamily homes line the graded hills. The city has adopted a controlled growth plan through the end of the century.

**70** *(left)* La Jolla Headlands

While waves pound these La Jolla cliffs, bathers can swim in a quiet cove just around the point. Red-roofed buildings in the distance across La Jolla Bay mark the La Jolla Beach and Tennis Club.

**71** Palm Canyon waterfall

Hikers climb from one boulder-rimmed pool to another high above Anza-Borrego's main campground. Watering holes support a small herd of rare bighorn sheep.

72  Tuna nets, San Diego Bay

Tugged into the air by the seiners' powerful winches, nets are draped onto the stern decks as crewmen check for damage.

73 *(right)* Sculpture, United States Courthouse

Artist Beverly Pepper's *Excalibur* spears the plaza across from the Wells Fargo Building. The low railing, a later addition by the city to discourage climbers, is still decried by art critics who loved the sculpture's uninterrupted joining of steel and concrete.

74 Koala bear, San Diego Zoo

No diet problem here; the koala's favorite food, eucalyptus leaves, is abundant in San Diego. The zoo may be best-known for its innovative natural habitats and landscaping—officials estimate the value of its plants as greater than that of its wildlife inhabitants.

75 *(right)* Orangutan, San Diego Zoo

A family of Sumatran orangutans, regal in their flowing coats, occupies one habitat in the zoo's new primate area.

76 *(left)* Navy ship at anchor, San Diego Bay
Home of the 11th Fleet, San Diego sees every
class of naval vessel. At sunset, the gray hull
of this ship shines like burnished copper; its
helicopter sits in shadow on an aft platform.

77 Bodysurfer, Del Mar
Waiting for the next onrush of waves, a lone
bodysurfer tries for just one more ride in the
70-degree summer water.

78 *(left)* Point Loma Lighthouse
The original lighthouse, built of brick rubble in 1855, was later found to be too high up in the fog banks and was replaced by a new light at the surf's edge.

79 Hanglider, Torrey Pines Cliffs
Banking on a wave of wind coming up the cliffs, this hanglider will soar back and forth parallel to the waves far below. The Glider Port, near University of California, San Diego, allows spectators a gull's-eye view.

80  Downtown seen from Point Loma

Shelter Island's marina bristles with masts surrounding the San Diego
Yacht Club. The distant skyline is several miles from the harbor mouth.

**81 Seaport Village Restaurant**
Stalking into the bay on ungainly legs, this Seaport Village seafood restaurant takes diners closer to the source. Catch of the day in San Diego is often swordfish or yellowtail.

**82 & 83** *(overleaf)* La Jolla
Viewed from Scenic Drive near the U.C.S.D. campus, the crescent shape of La Jolla Bay sweeps back from Alligator Head and the famous Cove.

**84** *(left)* Iceplant banks near
Windansea Beach

Lower tides expose small carpets of sand for
sunbathers beneath dazzling flowering iceplant.

**85** Epiphyllum 'Juniper'

Growing on tree trunks in the jungle wild,
these exotic 'orchid cactuses' have adapted
well to San Diego's climate as lathhouse and
indoor plants.

86  Coronado shorefishing

One ruined jetty breaks the sandy line of the Hotel Del Coronado's beach;
a perfect place to cast a line further into the surf—or try an ambitious line
or two on larger quarry.

**87** The *Star of India*, Maritime Museum

This square rigger's masts turn into San Diego's largest Christmas trees each holiday season. The old lumber schooner is berthed next to Anthony's Restaurant, a San Diego seafood tradition.

88 Tuna Fleet and Navy helicopter

Rising like praying mantises to snare a lone helicopter, these tuna boat masts reveal block and tackle assemblies strong enough to haul in tons of netted fish.